BEYOND THE COORDINATES

Unexplained Journeys in the Bermuda Triangle

Gordon Kean Clarke

S.D.N Publishing

Copyright © 2023 S.D.N Publishing

All rights reserved

The characters and events portrayed in this book are fictitious. Any similarity to real persons, living or dead, is coincidental and not intended by the author.

No part of this book may be reproduced, or stored in a retrieval system, or transmitted in any form or by any means, electronic, mechanical, photocopying, recording, or otherwise, without express written permission of the publisher.

ISBN: 9798871073926

CONTENTS

Title Page
Copyright
Disclaimer   1
Introduction: Where the Maps Diverge   4
Chapter 1: Into the Abyss   7
Chapter 2: Static Skies   11
Chapter 3: Grounded Dreams   15
Chapter 4: Beneath the Surface   18
Chapter 5: Submerged Secrets   21
Chapter 6: Tidal Changes   24
Chapter 7: Clockwork   27
Chapter 8: Adrift in the Continuum   31
Chapter 9: Unwound Futures   35
Chapter 10: Red Horizons   38
Chapter 11: Unfathomable Finds   41
Chapter 12: Ebbing Fortunes   44
Chapter 13: Star-Crossed   47
Chapter 14: Heavenly Phenomena   51
Chapter 15: Earthly Consequences   55
Chapter 16: A Quiet Prelude   58
Chapter 17: Notes in the Void   62

Chapter 18: Coda in Solitude	65
Conclusion	68
THE END	71

DISCLAIMER

The stories, characters, and events in this book are inspired by true events as recounted by those involved. However, it is essential for the reader to understand that all names, locations, timelines, and specific details have been altered to protect the privacy and identities of those who may have experienced events. Any resemblance to persons, living or dead, or other similar events or locales, is entirely coincidental.

While the narratives are inspired by reports and accounts that claim to involve unexplained phenomena, the book does not confirm the authenticity or veracity of these claims. Neither the author nor the publisher makes any guarantees regarding the factual accuracy or scientific reliability of the events described herein. The interpretations, opinions, and conclusions drawn in this book are those of the characters or the author's creative exploration and should not be understood as an endorsement of any theories, beliefs, or findings related to UFO or extraterrestrial phenomena.

Further, this book is not intended as a source of legal, medical, psychological, or scientific advice. The descriptions of law enforcement procedures, medical practices, or scientific methods and theories are for the purpose of storytelling and are not to be construed as being either complete or accurate. Experts in respective fields should be consulted for accurate information and guidance on such matters.

Moreover, the book may contain dialogues or descriptions that reflect the characters' beliefs, emotions, or states of mind, which should not be considered as a direct reflection of the author's or the publisher's viewpoints or opinions. This work aims to explore human experiences and perceptions in the context of unexplained phenomena, and it is not an attempt to validate or debunk any theories associated with the existence of UFOs, extraterrestrial life, or other paranormal activities.

The author and publisher expressly disclaim any liability for any direct, indirect, incidental, special, consequential, or exemplary damages, including but not limited to, damages for loss of profits, goodwill, use, data, or other intangible losses, resulting from the reading of this book. The reader is consuming the content of this book at their own risk and is responsible for their interpretation and use of any information provided.

By continuing to read this book, you acknowledge that you have read and understood this disclaimer, accepting that any expectation you may have of factual consistency or scientific rigor in the narratives is not the aim of this work. This book is intended solely for the purpose of entertainment, exploration, and artistic expression.

By proceeding beyond this point, you agree to absolve the author, the publisher, and all persons involved in the production and distribution of this book of any and all liability with respect to any emotional, psychological, or physical reactions or any other form of distress that you may experience during or after reading this book.

Enjoy the journey through the labyrinthine realms of the unexplained, but tread carefully—herein lies the territory of the unknown.

INTRODUCTION: WHERE THE MAPS DIVERGE

Even cartographers pause, their quills suspended in mid-air or their cursors hovering uncertainly, when sketching the lines that delineate an area we can only imperfectly describe. This is a territory marked as much by the depths of human fear and speculation as by the latitude and longitude coordinates that are its terrestrial identifiers. It is an area where the neat boundaries of our understanding blur into the ineffable and the arcane. Welcome to the Bermuda Triangle, a swath of ocean locked between Miami, Bermuda, and Puerto Rico. You are about to embark on a journey that will challenge the very limits of human comprehension and venture into the abyss of the unknown.

Navigational instruments falter here as if recoiling from an invisible force. Radios emit only static, a cacophonous choir drowning out cries for help. Planes vaporize from radar screens, and vessels vanish without trace, leaving behind them nothing but the eerie silence of an enigma. Time itself warps, becoming a viscous fluid in a realm that defies all known physics. This geographic triad has bemused, confounded, and terrified us for generations, but it continues to be a lodestar for adventurers and researchers, both professional and amateur alike. For what drives us into the maw of the unexplainable, if not the perpetual human urge to encounter and demystify the inexplicable?

This is a location imbued with the weight of countless tales, but herein we will delve into six specific narratives that disquietingly disrupt the very fibers of rational thought. These are not accounts bound by the contrivances of mere fiction or the artistic liberties of folklore; they resonate with the irrefutable gravity of personal experience, expert testimony, and rigorous investigation. In each of these six stories, individuals dare to confront the Bermuda Triangle, whether through scientific inquiry, mundane travel, or even unwitting misadventure. The outcomes of these confrontations are seldom what the protagonists expect and never what the paradigms of modern science can comfortably explain.

From aviators to marine biologists, from casual sailors to seasoned fishermen, from amateur astronomers to impassioned musicians—their fates converge at the same nebulous locus where the ordinary laws of space and time seem to be suspended in an eerie, disquieting stillness. These accounts do more than reveal the caprices of a particular geographic enigma; they raise unsettling questions about the boundaries of human understanding. For within the coordinates of the Bermuda Triangle, we all find ourselves adrift on waters that elude cartography, in an expansive, inscrutable void where our compasses spin aimlessly and the stars themselves seem to waver in the sky.

So, if you are prepared to contemplate the profound and the paradoxical, to entertain the confounding riddles that defy conventional wisdom, then venture forth. The stories that follow are an invitation—a beckoning from the deep, a call from beyond the fathomable corridors of our understanding. For in the Bermuda Triangle, you are not just confronting a geographical mystery; you are negotiating the very frontiers of existential disquiet. Here, you will meet people who were compelled, for one reason or another, to look over the edge of the known world, to stare into the enigmatic abyss, and to come back irreversibly changed—if they came back at all.

Prepare yourself: for you are about to journey beyond the coordinates, where the only certainty is the haunting refrain of the unexplained.

CHAPTER 1: INTO THE ABYSS

William "Bill" Thompson was anything but a novice when it came to aviation. With over two decades of experience, the subtle hum of an aircraft's engine felt more like a symphony to him—a blend of mechanical pitches that told a pilot everything they needed to know about the flying conditions. That partly explained his casual demeanor as he piloted his Cessna 172 Skyhawk over the Atlantic, closing in on the enigmatic coordinates collectively known as the Bermuda Triangle.

Instrumental Dissonance

Bill's journey started uneventfully. As he passed over the turquoise waters, he marveled at the placid sea reflecting the azure sky—a serenity he always sought to capture on his frequent solo flights. However, as he drew nearer to the heart of the Triangle, a discordant note struck his otherwise harmonious interaction with the plane. The aircraft's instruments began to behave erratically. His altimeter swung wildly, suggesting impossible variations in altitude within seconds. His magnetic compass, typically a rock-solid guide, started spinning as if possessed.

Bill ran through the emergency protocols in his mind, attempting to recalibrate the instruments manually. Despite his extensive training and an intimate familiarity with the Skyhawk, nothing seemed to revert the readings to normal. The radio static increased, gradually drowning the voices of air traffic controllers.

"Must be some sort of electrical interference," Bill mumbled to himself. His years of experience cautioned him not to jump to supernatural explanations. There had to be a logical reason for this. A magnetic anomaly, perhaps? Or some sort of atmospheric disturbance? The Bermuda Triangle was notorious for such phenomena, or so the legends said.

Ghostly Radio Signals

A crackling voice suddenly broke through the radio, dispersing his chain of thoughts. "November-Tango-Seven-Five-Four, do you read? You are off the plotted course. Please respond."

Bill quickly grabbed the radio, relief washing over him. "This is November-Tango-Seven-Five-Four. Experiencing instrumental malfunction. Request immediate assistance for rerouting."

A long pause ensued, punctuated only by bursts of static. When the voice returned, it was tinged with an inexplicable disquiet. "November-Tango-Seven-Five-Four, your last known position places you inside the designated high-risk zone. We advise you to climb to 10,000 feet and redirect your course by 45 degrees to the north-northeast."

The phrase "high-risk zone" resonated with Bill. Was this an official acknowledgment of the Bermuda Triangle's infamous reputation, or merely a procedural term? Regardless, he had no time to ponder; he needed to act. Gripping the controls firmly, he pushed the throttle to ascend.

The Final Broadcast

As the plane ascended, a sudden wave of unease washed over Bill. He felt as if he had penetrated an invisible veil, an intangible boundary separating the familiar world from one of unfathomable unpredictability. Just as he approached 10,000 feet, the radio emitted an ear-piercing screech, and then—silence.

His dashboard went dark, as if someone had flipped an off switch for the entire aircraft. Engine sputtering, Bill wrestled with the controls, trying to keep the plane level. The world outside seemed to blur, and for a moment, the horizon twisted into an unrecognizable swirl of colors. Then, just as suddenly as it had started, everything stopped.

Silence reigned. The controls went slack in his hands. His radio was dead. Bill found himself enveloped in an oppressive darkness, devoid of sound, sight, and orientation—a void where neither sky met sea nor sea met sky.

If a chilling thought crossed his mind—that he might not make it out of the Bermuda Triangle—it was a thought that never found voice. William "Bill" Thompson and his Cessna Skyhawk were never heard from again. He joined a long list of experienced pilots, intrepid mariners, and ordinary people who ventured into the Bermuda Triangle, only to vanish without a trace.

With Bill's disappearance, radio signals scoured the airwaves for any sign of his aircraft, navies patrolled the waters, and satellites skimmed the heavens. All endeavors proved fruitless. For Bill, the Bermuda Triangle became his final destination, a realm beyond the reach of latitude and longitude—a point of vanishing, perhaps forever.

The subsequent investigations, like so many before them, yielded no conclusive results, only raising more questions than answers.

What had he encountered in those last moments? Was it a fluke of nature, a technological glitch, or something more arcane? As with so many who had disappeared within these enigmatic coordinates, the answers lay hidden, swallowed by the insatiable mystery that is the Bermuda Triangle.

CHAPTER 2: STATIC SKIES

The disappearance of William's aircraft threw ripples across several spheres of human endeavor. At once, it was a matter of professional concern for air traffic controllers, the nub of intrigue for government investigators, and the kernel of countless rumors and conspiracy theories that ever swirl around the Bermuda Triangle. The mystery was as perplexing as it was perturbing: an experienced pilot, aboard a well-maintained private plane, seemingly vanishes off the radar.

The Phantom Plane on Radar Screens

The perplexity of William's disappearance can be better appreciated when we consider the sequence of events from the perspective of air traffic control. On the night of the event, when William's Cessna first began to wobble and dip erratically, the air traffic controllers had initially presumed it to be temporary instrument failure on their end. Frantic recalibrations and double-checks quickly disabused them of that notion. All other aircraft in the region were transmitting data impeccably. The issue was isolated to William's plane alone. Controllers attempted repeated radio contact, following standard protocol, but were met with nothing but a wall of unyielding static.

It was then that an inexplicable phenomenon occurred. For a fleeting moment, lasting no more than a few seconds, William's aircraft blinked back onto the radar. Its location, speed, and altitude readings, however, defied logic. According to the data, the plane was at an altitude of 30,000 feet—well beyond the Cessna's service ceiling—traveling at speeds in excess of Mach 1, an impossibility for the small aircraft. And then, as suddenly as it had appeared, the plane vanished from the radar, leaving only an imprint of electronic gibberish in its wake.

Initial Government Investigations

The disappearance engaged the immediate attention of various governmental agencies, including the Federal Aviation Administration (FAA) and the National Transportation Safety Board (NTSB), which in turn sought support from the Department of Defense. A classified inquiry was convened to delve into the anomaly, considering the potential national security implications. This was no mere missing aircraft; this was an aircraft that had behaved in ways contrary to known physical laws.

Flight data recorders and cockpit voice recorders, usually referred to as black boxes, are generally invaluable in unraveling aviation mysteries. However, William's aircraft was not equipped with a black box—its installation is not mandatory for small private planes—which rendered conventional investigative avenues fruitless. Satellite images provided no leads either; weather conditions had been almost idyllic, with only a few insignificant cloud formations. Thus, the initial reports, heavily redacted upon public release, ambiguously concluded that the plane was "unrecoverable under unknown circumstances."

Simultaneously, a covert investigation looked into William's personal and financial records, following the less glamorous, yet often revealing, leads. Was he under financial stress? Was this an elaborate ruse to disappear and start anew? All such hypotheses were gradually eroded by the weight of negative evidence. William had a stable job, a loving family, and no discernible motive to vanish intentionally.

The Nexus of Unexplained Phenomena

As months turned into years, William's case found its place in the annals of Bermuda Triangle mysteries, a compendium of cases shrouded in enigma and speculation. Aviation experts, marine biologists, and meteorologists, despite their diverse viewpoints and theoretical frameworks, failed to provide an integrative explanation. The case also spurred debates in more esoteric circles: those who ardently discuss the existence of underwater alien bases, portals to parallel universes, or vortexes that bend time and space. Yet, the tangible evidence to substantiate such theories remains ever elusive.

Despite the plethora of investigations and the confluence of interdisciplinary expertise, the whereabouts of William's aircraft remain unknown. His disappearance continues to perplex the rational mind and stoke the imaginative fires of those intrigued by the Bermuda Triangle. The last radio contact, a melding of static and distorted human voice, provides no answers but echoes as a haunting refrain in the labyrinthine corridors of unsolved mysteries.

In the absence of conclusive evidence, all that remains is an unsettling quietude. William's plane never returned, the government agencies eventually relegated the case to their cold case files, and the incongruent radar data were archived as an "anomalous event" among countless others. Yet, the questions linger, hanging in the air like an unresolved chord in a symphonic movement. What really happened in those moments when the aircraft vanished? What explains its paradoxical readings? And where, in the endless expanse of ocean and sky, did William go?

GORDON KEAN CLARKE

Some questions, it seems, remain unanswerable, as if taunting our quest for understanding, compelling us to acknowledge the limits of human rationality.

CHAPTER 3: GROUNDED DREAMS

An Open Sky with No Landing

The day William vanished, the ripple effects were like a sonic boom, disorienting and cacophonous in their resonance. As a seasoned pilot, William had always been the family's anchor, a steady force in a world perpetually spinning out of control. But the Bermuda Triangle had swallowed him up without even the courtesy of a debris trail. From air traffic control to navy operations, everyone was baffled. Hundreds of square miles were scoured, both above and beneath the waves, but not a single clue floated to the surface. It was as if he had vaporized into the very ether he flew through.

After a thorough examination of flight records, radar anomalies, and military intelligence, the governmental inquiry ended as a file in a bureaucratic labyrinth. This was just another Bermuda Triangle case: unexplainable, unprovable, and unsettling. But to William's family, the consequences were inescapable.

The Unraveling Knots of Matrimony

In the weeks that followed, William's wife, Grace, oscillated between fragile hope and piercing despair. As days turned into months, something inside her began to break. She felt betrayed, abandoned. Whispers circulated in their tight-knit community: had William disappeared intentionally? Was he tired of the suburban stability, the monotonous responsibility of family life? The more the idea was voiced, the more it gnawed at Grace's psyche.

The last straw was a package that arrived six months after William's disappearance. It was a trove of Bermuda Triangle conspiracy theories, books, and documentaries that William had ordered weeks before his ill-fated flight. Although William had always been a rational man, the allure of the Bermuda Triangle had drawn him into a labyrinth of obsessions he had carefully hidden. Grace, already contending with spirals of doubt, felt her worldview crumble. The divorce papers were filed in a somber haze of legal formalities. Grace wanted to be free of the haunting questions, even if it meant carrying the weight of unanswered ones.

A Generational Obsession

Jason, William's teenage son, internalized his father's disappearance differently. At an age when young men are discovering their identities, Jason felt the vacuum left by his father as an existential chasm. While Grace sought emotional distance from the Bermuda Triangle, Jason gravitated toward it like a moth to a flame. The mysterious package that had broken his mother's resolve became his arcane treasure trove.

As Jason scoured the books and examined theories—from magnetic anomalies to underwater extraterrestrial bases—he felt his skepticism dissolving. College became an afterthought; instead, he enrolled in flight school. The instructors noticed his relentless focus. Yet, they also noted a dangerous edge to his daring—a boundary-pushing mentality that had them worried. Despite the concerns, Jason's academic performance was exemplary, a testament to an obsession honed to razor-sharp focus.

The culmination of his preoccupation came when he was finally licensed to fly. He acquired a small plane, equipped with the latest technology. Though his family protested, Jason's mind was made up; he would enter the Bermuda Triangle to find what had eluded others. Whether it was answers or his father he found, Jason was unyielding in his quest.

The Horizon Ahead

William's disappearance became more than a mystery; it metamorphosed into a familial schism that severed emotional ties and led two loved ones down divergent paths. While Grace looked for closure in the finality of legal documents, choosing to place her faith in the harsh reality of absence, Jason chose an ambiguous but alluring horizon, one that could either vindicate his father's legacy or consume him just as it had William.

The story of William's disappearance might have ended for the government and for the legions of amateur sleuths who populate internet forums, but for his family, it was an ongoing narrative with no resolution in sight. The Bermuda Triangle's enigmatic allure had proven to be an intergenerational snare, entrapping both father and son in its confounding maze. Whether either would find a way out—or simply add to the Triangle's legend—was a question for the gods of fate and the restless spirits that some say haunt those enigmatic waters.

CHAPTER 4: BENEATH THE SURFACE

The Allure of the Abyss

Emily Dalton, a skilled marine biologist, always had an unquenchable curiosity for the enigmatic. Her most recent project led her to study ocean currents in the Bermuda Triangle, a place saturated with mystery and speculation. Focused on her scientific observations, Emily had never given credence to the region's perplexing reputation—until she discovered an underwater cave, uncharted and surreptitious, calling to her like a siren's song. Encased in her diving suit and armed with research instruments, Emily entered the cave, not knowing her life was about to change irrevocably.

A Timeless Odyssey

As she swam deeper into the cave, the aura changed dramatically. The blue aquatic expanse turned into a pitch-black void. Her torchlight flickered erratically, casting eerie shadows on the rock formations. Her instruments, designed to record temperature, pressure, and time, displayed jumbled data, as if disrupted by an invisible force. Though a seasoned diver, Emily felt a palpable sense of disorientation, as though the cave were distorting her perception of time and space.

With every stroke, Emily felt like she was moving farther from the reality she knew. She had planned to spend 30 minutes in the cave, yet her perception of time warped, making it impossible to discern minutes from hours. The cave seemed to expand and contract, alternately vast like a cathedral and then constricting, like a throat ready to swallow her whole. Shadows took on sinuous shapes, almost like guardians warning her of some cosmic secret. And then she heard it—a faint resonance, a low-frequency hum emanating from the belly of the cave, a sound so deep it was almost felt rather than heard.

Curiously, Emily tried to capture the mysterious phenomena using her recording equipment. But every attempt was thwarted; all devices malfunctioned, as if the cave itself rejected empirical scrutiny. Yet, her skin tingled, sensing an electrifying, almost spiritual, undercurrent in the water. It was as if the cave harbored its own life force, protecting its arcane knowledge from the prying eyes of science.

The Intervention of Science and Navy

Upon surfacing, Emily immediately contacted her research team to document this inexplicable experience. Yet, despite her meticulous descriptions, the cave remained elusive, as though purposefully evading detection. A team of Navy divers was dispatched, employing advanced sonar mapping technologies. But as they swam through the coordinates Emily provided, they found nothing but open water—the cave had vanished as if it never existed.

Cognizant of the Bermuda Triangle's notorious reputation, the scientific community became deeply interested in Emily's findings—or lack thereof. Oceanographers, geologists, and even a few individuals from governmental agencies descended upon the area to conduct a battery of tests. Yet, all data proved inconclusive.

As for the Navy, the subsequent investigations were kept under a veil of confidentiality. It was rumored that they employed advanced submersibles to scour the depths, perhaps even using experimental technology that could "see" through the distortions that had thwarted Emily's instruments. However, no official report was ever released, and Emily's discovery remained an inexplicable mystery.

An Intellectual Pariah

As weeks turned into months, Emily became a subject of both fascination and skepticism within the scientific community. Despite her rigorous documentation, colleagues began to question her credibility. Could a marine biologist of her repute fabricate such an outlandish tale? Her research grant was rescinded, and academic journals rescinded their offer to publish her findings, citing insufficient evidence. Yet, Emily remained steadfast in her conviction that she had experienced an extraordinary phenomenon.

Although her professional credibility waned, Emily felt an inexorable pull back to the waters of the Bermuda Triangle, almost as if the cave—or whatever force resided within it—was calling her back to uncover its hidden mysteries.

Summary

In an ironic twist of fate, Emily Dalton, once a paragon of scientific objectivity, became the embodiment of the Bermuda Triangle's enduring enigma. Her academic downfall was precipitated not by a lack of expertise or commitment but by an experience so profound, yet so resistant to scientific explanation, that it shook the very foundations of her understanding. Stripped of her academic mantle, but invigorated by a mysterious connection to an inexplicable phenomenon, Emily's life became a paradox, much like the Bermuda Triangle itself—an impenetrable mystery defiant of human understanding.

CHAPTER 5: SUBMERGED SECRETS

The atmosphere inside the underwater cave was at once disorienting and tranquil, as if the very water molecules had conspired to forge an uncanny calm. Emily's high-powered underwater flashlight cut through the gloom, illuminating the intricate stalactites that hung down from the cave ceiling like chandeliers in a gothic cathedral. She had stumbled upon an aquatic marvel, a sanctuary sculpted by the relentless currents and pressures that the Bermuda Triangle harbored.

The Labyrinthine Cave

It was a maze of labyrinthine tunnels and chambers, each more convoluted than the last. The cave system seemed to stretch for miles, wrapping around itself like an underwater Gordian Knot. Emily felt as though she were navigating through a liquid dream, her perceptions blurred at the edges. What was most confounding was the absolute absence of marine life. There were no fish darting about, no coral structures pulsating with colors—just an eerie silence that made her own heartbeat resound in her ears like a monotonous drumbeat.

Emily had activated her high-tech submersible GPS to map the cave's topology. But as she made her way deeper, she noticed the screen flickering, the digital map contorting and distorting as if mirroring the cave's enigmatic geometry. Within moments, the device malfunctioned completely, leaving her to rely solely on her intuition and the luminescent paint markers she had brought along.

The Vanishing Data

Intending to record this uncharted realm for scientific scrutiny, Emily drew samples of the water and took numerous photographs with her underwater camera. But as she reviewed the captured images on her camera's screen, she was taken aback. The photographs displayed nothing but indistinct blurs and unrecognizable shapes. Frowning, she tried to record a video, only for the camera to shut off abruptly, its battery inexplicably drained. Her sophisticated equipment, designed to operate in the harshest marine environments, had met its match in this cave.

Emily, who had always approached the natural world through the lens of empiricism, was thrown into a state of cognitive dissonance. Her instruments failed her, data eluded capture, and the material world felt incorporeal, almost ephemeral. The more she tried to scrutinize her surroundings, the more elusive they became. Time itself felt distorted; minutes seemed to stretch into hours, yet she had no way to measure the passage of time. Her watch had stopped functioning as well.

Government and Scientific Involvement

Two days after Emily emerged from her aquatic ordeal, a Naval research vessel, alerted by her team, arrived at the coordinates of the underwater cave. Advanced sonar equipment was deployed, and a team of Navy divers was sent in, but they couldn't locate the cave's entrance. As if mocking human endeavor, the cave had vanished—or perhaps it had never existed in the material sense that Emily had believed.

Simultaneously, laboratories tasked with analyzing Emily's water samples found them to be identical to the surrounding ocean, as if she had never ventured into the cave. An interdisciplinary scientific committee, comprising marine biologists, geologists, and oceanographers, convened to examine her case. Their ultimate conclusion was disconcerting: Emily had experienced "oceanic disorientation," a psychologically-induced perceptual anomaly exacerbated by nitrogen narcosis, a condition that could affect divers. They ruled out equipment failure, attributing the malfunctions to user error.

Emily found herself thrust into the unenviable position of defending her sanity and professional credibility. She was marginalized within the scientific community and became an object of media scrutiny. Amid speculations and conspiracy theories, her research grants were revoked, and she was unceremoniously removed from ongoing projects.

However, as her professional life crumbled, Emily began to experience a series of vivid, almost transcendental dreams where she was back in the cave. Instead of inducing terror, these nocturnal visits filled her with an ineffable sense of serenity and a profound spiritual connection to the ocean—emotions she had never before associated with her scientific pursuits.

In the end, the cave remained an enigma, its secrets as elusive as the ever-shifting currents of the Bermuda Triangle. It had left Emily with more questions than answers, unraveling her conventional understanding of the natural world and forcing her into the murky waters of metaphysical speculation. As much as the Bermuda Triangle had swallowed planes and ships, it had now consumed her rational worldview, leaving her to ponder the ineffable mysteries lurking in the depths of the ocean—and perhaps, within herself.

CHAPTER 6: TIDAL CHANGES

The Price of Inquiry

In the ensuing months after her bewildering experience within the uncharted underwater cave, Emily Brant found herself grappling with a disquieting sense of fragmentation. Her perceptions of time, once linear and certain, now ebbed and flowed in unpredictable tidal surges. Memory lapses became more frequent, swamping her with unease as precious minutes, hours, even entire days seemed to vanish from her conscious recollection.

Colleagues took note of her increasingly erratic behavior, ranging from nonsensical ramblings about the "hidden geometry" of the ocean floor to her sudden disinterest in conventional scientific inquiry. Observers found her vexing blend of pseudo-scientific mysticism and moments of profound lucidity both fascinating and disturbing, reminiscent of a modern-day Cassandra with her apocalyptic pronouncements on marine ecology.

A Reckoning in Academia

The academic ramifications were swift and severe. The National Oceanic and Atmospheric Administration (NOAA) revoked her research grant, citing concerns over "questionable methodology" and "mental fitness for rigorous scientific research." Her deteriorating reputation further weakened her chances of recovering any semblance of academic credibility. Even the navy, which had initially shown interest in her cave findings, now treated her accounts with a palpable skepticism bordering on disdain. Where once she had been a subject of discussion in scientific circles, her name now elicited eye-rolls and hushed whispers.

As one door closed, however, another opened, albeit in the esoteric realm of oceanic spirituality. Disenfranchised by mainstream science, Emily began to explore alternative perspectives, from the theosophical teachings of Blavatsky to Taoist philosophies connecting water to the very essence of existence. Although dismissed by some as a descent into quackery, others perceived in Emily a renewed focus, an almost religious dedication to uncovering the ineffable mysteries she believed lay at the heart of the Bermuda Triangle.

An Unlikely Sanctuary

Emily's newfound spiritual convictions led her to join the community of eco-activists and oceanic spiritualists, often sharing her experiences at forums that regarded the Bermuda Triangle as a vortex of ancient energies. Paradoxically, her unscientific claims found their most ardent supporters among those who mistrusted or rejected scientific rationalism altogether.

During one such gathering, she met Evelyn, a marine conservationist who held a holistic view of ocean preservation. Evelyn recognized in Emily a kindred spirit, their connection deepening despite—or perhaps because of—their shared experiences of professional marginalization. Together, they launched a series of small-scale projects aimed at harnessing "natural oceanic energies" for environmental healing, an endeavor that blended quasi-science with indigenous wisdom. Though far from the conventional marine biology that Emily had been trained in, this path offered a semblance of purpose and stability, an intellectual sanctuary amid the turbulence of her life.

However, questions remained unanswered. While her academic career was essentially extinguished, her spiritual flame had been ignited. Yet the ineffable events that transpired within the subterranean realm of the Bermuda Triangle continued to haunt her. Were they figments of her imagination, delusions induced by nitrogen narcosis, or could they indeed be fragments of a greater cosmic puzzle? Each question bred others, confounding the boundary between empirical observation and subjective experience, between sanity and madness.

Summary

In the aftermath of her Bermuda Triangle episode, Emily Brant's professional life underwent a transformation as dramatic as her personal metamorphosis. Alienated from the scientific community due to her unconventional theories and inexplicable behavioral changes, she faced personal and academic ruin. However, she found an unexpected haven among oceanic spiritualists and eco-activists, where her strange tales found receptive ears. In pursuing this less-traveled path, she discovered a new form of connection to the ocean—a spiritual one, saturated with mysticism and rife with unanswered questions. Though she lost much, her restless search for understanding continued, now propelled by a cryptic sense of destiny, a yearning to decipher the unfathomable equations of the sea, whose solutions, if they existed, eluded not only her but humanity at large.

CHAPTER 7: CLOCKWORK

Tom and Linda stared out at the sapphire sea, completely enamored with the idea that they were alone on this boat in the Bermuda Triangle. This anniversary trip was supposed to be a celebratory experience—time away from the incessant digital deluge and the overwhelming responsibilities back home. They had been warned, even lightly mocked by friends and family for choosing such a location. But Tom, ever the romantic, wanted to take his spouse somewhere unforgettable.

A Change in the Sea

As Tom steadied the sail, Linda noticed something unusual on the GPS. A whirlpool was forming just a few hundred meters away from their location, almost imperceptibly at first but then with increasing ferocity. The phenomenon was too anomalous to be purely meteorological. No storm clouds were in sight, and the weather had been extraordinarily calm.

Feeling the boat pull towards the whirling mass of water, Tom immediately set the vessel's engine to full throttle in an attempt to escape its pull. It was too late; they were caught in the strange vortex. An electrifying sensation filled the air, making the hairs on their arms stand on end. The atmosphere turned heavy, as if compressed by an invisible force. A low humming reverberated through the boat, inaudible at first, but gradually intensifying into a resonance that seemed to tremble in the core of their beings.

A Riddle in Time

Once clear of the whirlpool, a sense of disorientation washed over Tom and Linda. Stunned, they checked the GPS, expecting it to be malfunctioning. However, what they saw transcended the scope of any technological glitch; the date displayed was not just inaccurate, it was impossible. The screen showed a date nearly ten years into the future. Confusion morphed into incredulity. Even the celestial bodies seemed dislocated, the positions of the stars askew as if a cartographer of the heavens had made a glaring error.

Attempting to radio for help, they found that their equipment was eerily silent. No static, no voices, nothing. As they scoured the frequencies, the unsettling truth began to unfold: they were isolated in a way that was both spatially and temporally incongruous. Their surroundings were the same, but the coordinates of time had shifted—like characters in a narrative who find themselves inexplicably transplanted into another chapter.

The Interlude

The couple spent what felt like hours, though they couldn't be sure, trying to readjust their equipment and make sense of the charts. Yet every instrument they consulted corroborated the enigma; they were adrift in a lacuna of time. Even the ocean seemed to be a different hue, an otherworldly shade that defied natural explanation. Tom and Linda looked at each other, their eyes windows to an internal landscape of bewilderment and mounting dread. Words failed them. The very fabric of their reality had been perforated, and they were peering into the void beyond.

Then, as abruptly as it had started, another jolt went through the boat. It was as if they had passed through an invisible barrier. The atmosphere lightened, the unnatural heaviness lifting like a fog. With apprehension, they checked their instruments again. The GPS now displayed the correct date. Their radio buzzed back to life, filled with the routine chatter of nearby vessels and weather updates. The stars above resumed their familiar constellations. It was as if they had been spat back into their original timeline, like wayward detritus expelled from the maw of some cosmic anomaly.

However, the impact of this otherworldly episode did not fade as quickly as it had arrived. As they continued to sail, something unspoken weighed on them both—a dissonance in the harmony of their relationship. Linda felt an inexplicable urge to jot down their experience in her journal, despite her hands trembling as she wrote. Tom, on the other hand, became consumed by a torrent of questions that gnawed at his understanding of reality.

In that uncanny episode, the veneer of the world had been peeled back to expose a tangle of quantum threads, an ontological snarl that neither of them had the lexicon to articulate. They were haunted by a paradox: the sense that this voyage, originally intended to draw them closer, had inserted an unfathomable distance between them, stretching far beyond the three dimensions they could perceive.

While they could not comprehend what had transpired, they both knew, deep within their cognizance, that they had witnessed something that defied explanation—a phenomenon that would require a paradigm shift to even begin to understand. How do you return to the pedestrian realm of deadlines and groceries after that? They stared at the horizon, contemplating a future that suddenly felt as inscrutable as the depths they had just narrowly escaped.

As the boat sailed onward, leaving behind waters that were no longer just a physical space but also an enigma wrapped in coordinates and time, Tom and Linda realized that their lives had been irreversibly altered. While the GPS could now find their geographical location, locating their place in the intricate design of existence seemed, at least for the moment, utterly beyond reach.

CHAPTER 8: ADRIFT IN THE CONTINUUM

The Lost Time

The yacht, piloted by Tom and Linda, a couple celebrating their anniversary, bobbed and swayed in a turmoil of water and weather. The whirlpool that had suddenly appeared beneath them seemed to mock all laws of physics, contorting the waves into monstrous loops. The experience defied simple metaphors; it was as if the ocean itself had turned into a Möbius strip, challenging the conventional perception of space and time.

What was stranger still was their GPS, which now displayed a date that was impossible—two years into the future. All the data points and satellite navigation couldn't explain the baffling temporal dislocation. The couple stared at each other, suspended in disbelief. They tried to confirm their situation by checking their phones, but the devices were disoriented, fluctuating between time zones, years, and even decades, before finally shutting down.

"Is this real?" Tom whispered, his voice tinged with a terror that only utter incomprehensibility can inspire. Linda looked at him but couldn't formulate a reply. They were lost, adrift in the continuum of time and space, guided by no compass—literal or metaphorical—that they understood.

Witnesses and Shadows

Their predicament would have continued to be their private horror if it weren't for the group of fishermen near the Bermuda Triangle, who witnessed something extraordinary. They had seen Tom and Linda's yacht vanish right in front of them, enveloped by a whirlpool, only to reappear minutes later in the same spot, though the whirlpool was gone as if it never existed. "Like a ghost ship, it was," said one fisherman during an interview, his eyes wide with a blend of awe and dread. "It was there, then it wasn't, and then it was there again."

Word got out, and soon maritime authorities were involved. Subpoenas were issued, naval inspections conducted, and satellite data reviewed. However, all the trappings of an official inquiry couldn't solve the mystery. Tom and Linda were extensively questioned, their yacht was examined down to the last bolt, and even the oceanic currents were studied, yet nothing yielded an explanation. Then, the government stepped in. Classified stamps were affixed to their case files, and nondisclosure agreements were handed out like candy on Halloween. The fishermen who had witnessed the event were warned not to speak about it, under the dubious claim of "national security."

Reality Redacted

As days turned into weeks, Tom and Linda found their lives being disassembled, bit by bit. Neither the clinical decorum of government agents nor the zeal of conspiracy theorists who sought them out for interviews did anything to shed light on their surreal experience. In whispers, they discussed what had happened, yet were too frightened to delve into it. It was as though speaking it out loud would make it more real and therefore, more terrifying. Each night they would check the date on their phones before going to bed and each morning on waking up, half-expecting to find themselves lost in another twist of time.

Tom began to research temporal anomalies, wormholes, and theories of relativity. He wanted answers, and conventional science was not providing them. He dug deep into the esoterica of quantum mechanics, flirting with the fringes of scientific respectability.

Linda, however, chose a different path. She started to write, putting their experiences into words. At first, it was a form of catharsis, an attempt to make sense of what had happened. Yet, as she wrote, she realized that her work might serve a dual purpose. If she couldn't understand the phenomena, she could at least document it. Linda thought that somewhere in her writing might lie the key to the questions that haunted them.

The government investigation into their case yielded no official results. The documents pertaining to their experience were eventually sealed, buried somewhere under the labyrinthine bureaucracy of a nondescript agency. However, for Tom and Linda, there was no sealing away the memories, no bureaucracy that could archive their haunting questions. Each was left with an abyss that neither science nor reason could fill. Tom's quest for truth led him further away from the world he once knew, spiraling him into realms of speculations and shadows. Linda's documentation of their ordeal became a book, a tome of disturbing questions rather than comforting answers. It earned her both public acclaim and professional skepticism.

Their shared experience in the Bermuda Triangle had unmoored them from the reality they had known, casting them adrift on unsettling currents of time and possibility. While their external world remained deceptively unchanged, their internal worlds had been altered, unrecognizable from the lives they lived before. Tom and Linda now navigated a world imbued with hidden meanings and obscured truths, a reality permanently distorted by the whirlpool that still swirled silently, unseen, in the depths of their minds.

CHAPTER 9: UNWOUND FUTURES

The Aftermath

No one could dispute the paradoxical nature of Tom and Linda's experience within the Bermuda Triangle. That inexplicable whirlpool, the momentary dislocation of time and space, and then their sudden reappearance; it had defied the principles of causality that our universe is so fondly hinged upon. The couple found themselves unscathed but irrevocably changed, their shared existence now tinted by the uncanny and the unknown.

Tom's Conspiracy Cloud

Tom, who had once been a man of science, with a rational explanation for nearly everything, found himself inexorably drawn to the web of conspiracy theories that surround the Bermuda Triangle. He spent long hours researching classified documents, testimonies, and other reported incidents. It was as if the Bermuda Triangle had ingested a part of his skepticism and, in return, regurgitated a quasi-religious believer of high strangeness.

Friends and family grew concerned as he became increasingly introverted, obsessed with esoteric theories, and began contributing to online forums under pseudonyms like "TemporalSailor" and "VortexRider." Tom wrote long articles, advocating theories ranging from interdimensional portals to classified government experiments that manipulated the spacetime fabric itself. However, even as he gained a considerable following among like-minded individuals, his obsession cost him his career and, more painfully, his relationship with Linda.

Linda's Literary Catharsis

Linda, conversely, sought solace and understanding through articulation. She wrote a memoir about their unsettling journey, cleverly titled "Anomalies of the Deep: A Love Story Adrift in Time." The book delved into the psychology of extraordinary experiences, the elasticity of time, and the impact it had on their marriage. Linda consulted with physicists, marine biologists, and even experts in the field of psychology to give her narrative both scientific and emotional gravity.

Surprisingly, or perhaps inevitably, her book became a bestseller. Academic scholars cited it as a layperson's insight into temporal dislocation theories, while literary critics hailed it as an honest exploration of emotional dislocation within relationships. However, the accolades and the attention were not without a price. The recounting of the mysterious event had opened a wellspring of anxieties she had long suppressed. Though she went on lecture tours and attended seminars, she found herself battling an anxiety disorder that manifested in inexplicable panic attacks, especially when close to any body of water.

Unresolved Tensions and Unanswered Questions

The government's role in the whole affair was notably ambiguous. After the initial media spectacle, there was a conspicuous and rapid fading of their story from the news cycle. Requests for interviews and investigative reports were inexplicably halted, replaced by articles that questioned the credibility of Tom and Linda. It was as though there was a subtle, yet concerted, effort to smudge their story into the realm of urban legends, a contemporary cautionary tale that one talks about in hushed tones but never takes too seriously.

It was impossible to discern if Tom and Linda were victims of an enigmatic phenomenon or subjects of an elaborately crafted disinformation campaign. Their marriage crumbled under the weight of their divergent coping mechanisms—Tom's spiraling descent into conspiratorial maelstroms and Linda's public unpacking of their private abyss. Both sought answers in their respective ways, and both were left with a haunting incompleteness, a yearning that could not be satiated by any explanation, scientific or speculative.

Their life trajectories had been altered, much like the ripples created by a stone thrown into a pond, radiating outward but never quite settling. The Bermuda Triangle had been their stone, and they were the ripples, their lives forever oscillating between what was known and what could never be understood. And so, they moved forward, apart yet forever linked by an event that transcended the boundaries of reason and ventured into the fringes of the inexplicable.

CHAPTER 10: RED HORIZONS

Carlos had always been inextricably tied to the sea. As a fisherman who had spent more time on water than on land, he had heard myriad tales about the Bermuda Triangle. But for him, the enigmatic region of ocean had been a lucrative fishing ground, a generous provider. Little did he know that his perceptions would soon be clouded with questions more intricate than any fishing net he'd ever cast.

The Sanguine Sea

On an overcast afternoon, Carlos guided his trawler through the familiar waters of the Atlantic. His instincts, honed through years of maritime experience, told him this was the spot—the fishing ground rich in piscatorial bounties. He cast his net into the deep blue and settled in for what he presumed would be a routine haul.

When he began pulling the net back up, he felt an unprecedented resistance. It was as if the sea were actively fighting his efforts. The water around the boat churned, a bizarre tinge of red filling the froth. Startled, Carlos released a portion of the net, slackening it just enough to pull it aboard. The red waters churned in his wake, as if agitated by some subaqueous force.

The Enigmatic Artifact

When the net finally surfaced, Carlos was taken aback not by the volume of his catch but by an oddity entangled within it—an artifact. It was an oblong object, partially encased in coral, but clearly not of natural origin. It bore inscriptions in a language foreign to both the eye and the intellect, akin to undulating lines that seemed almost—animated.

Eager yet wary, Carlos detached it carefully from the net and placed it in an insulated box. The red water around him seemed to recede, as if yielding to the artifact's removal. Intrigued but baffled, Carlos charted a course back to the mainland, a series of questions roiling through his mind. Was the artifact related to the legends of the Bermuda Triangle, or was this yet another enigma born out of its elusive depths?

Repercussions and Speculations

As soon as Carlos docked, he contacted several marine researchers, cultural anthropologists, and linguistic experts. Each one was more perplexed than the last, deferring to higher echelons of expertise. The artifact soon caught the attention of governmental agencies. After a cursory examination, they classified it as an "object of unknown provenance" and transported it to a high-security research facility.

Within hours, social media was awash with speculations. Some contended it was proof of Atlantis, while others suggested it was an alien beacon. But what unsettled Carlos the most was the hue of the waters from which it was extracted. Tests indicated the red was not algae or any known form of marine life. It was as if the ocean had bled.

Sitting in the solemnity of his trawler, Carlos reflected on the unfolding enigma. His simple fishing expedition had turned into an odyssey of unknown realms—realms where the linearity of human comprehension warped into incomprehensible curvature.

No amount of maritime lore could offer him guidance now. He was, both metaphorically and literally, in uncharted waters.

So ends the introduction to the curious tale of Carlos, the fisherman who pulled more than fish from the depths of the Bermuda Triangle. His life was about to transition from the mundane to the inexplicable, as scrutiny intensified and the artifact's inexplicable disappearance from the secured lab left more questions than answers. Would Carlos ever find his bearings in a world whose dimensions had expanded far beyond the nautical miles he knew so well? Only time would unfold the layers of this ever-deepening mystery, a testament to the ceaseless enigma that is the Bermuda Triangle.

CHAPTER 11: UNFATHOMABLE FINDS

The Artifact in Question

Carlos stared in awe at the object now resting on the deck of his boat—a complex, geometric artifact shimmering with an iridescent sheen. It was unlike anything he'd ever seen, defying description with its seemingly alien aesthetic. After taking dozens of photographs and making sure to store it carefully, Carlos returned to shore, his mind ablaze with speculation. The local maritime authority and an interdisciplinary team of scientists were immediately interested.

Geologists were initially in favor of a mineralogical origin, considering the composition of the artifact: an amalgamation of quartz-like material and metals not naturally found in the Earth's crust. The object was sent to a high-security lab for radiometric dating, spectral analysis, and a battery of other tests. Intriguingly, the radiometric dating was inconclusive, presenting data that suggested the artifact was either incredibly ancient or so recent that it essentially disrupted the efficacy of the technique itself. Moreover, metallurgists and crystallographers found themselves perplexed by the way the metallic portions of the object seemed to flow and merge with the crystalline sections, displaying a kind of unity between materials usually considered disparate in nature.

Vanishing Act and International Fallout

The significance of the artifact was not lost on international observers. The news had traveled beyond national borders, attracting the scrutiny of governments and scientific institutions worldwide. Within the labyrinthine chambers of the United Nations, there were murmurs of it being a potential "OOPArt" (Out-of-Place Artifact), an acronym often used to denote anachronistic and mystifying objects discovered in geological strata where they ostensibly do not belong. Even the Vatican showed interest, dispatching a delegation of religious scholars and scientists to examine this enigmatic find.

However, the artifact would soon become more enigmatic than anyone had anticipated. In a turn of events that could only be described as Kafkaesque, the artifact vanished from its maximum-security lab, bypassing state-of-the-art surveillance and biometric access controls. Investigators were dumbfounded, for no trace of unauthorized entry or manipulation could be discerned. The disappearance of the artifact soured diplomatic relations among several countries, with accusations of theft, sabotage, and espionage becoming topics of heated international discourse. Some even suggested that the artifact's disappearance was a manipulation to distract from more pressing geopolitical issues, though such conjectures remained in the realm of speculative theories and ideological blogs.

Carlos: From Fisherman to Pariah

In the immediate aftermath of the artifact's disappearance, Carlos found himself at the epicenter of a swirling vortex of skepticism and vilification. The local maritime authority revoked his fishing license, citing his potential involvement in a case of "scientific fraud and deception." They posited that Carlos may have orchestrated the entire episode, fabricating the artifact to gain attention or perhaps to influence commodity prices for some insidious financial gain. Local media, once fascinated by his story, now portrayed him as a charlatan. The once-affable fisherman found himself a pariah in his community, receiving glares instead of greetings when he walked through the streets.

However, there were those who remained intrigued by Carlos' experience and vouched for his integrity. Local universities invited him to give talks about his encounter in the Bermuda Triangle, and a growing counterculture saw him as a man suppressed by a consortium of mainstream scientific institutions and governments. Soon, Carlos found a new niche—as a tour guide for expeditions into the Bermuda Triangle, detailing his experience and providing firsthand accounts to eager adventurers and truth-seekers.

In a world inclined towards skepticism, the artifact—whether it ever existed in the corporeal sense or not—had vanished, leaving in its wake a cacophony of theories, accusations, and unanswered questions. As for Carlos, his journey had taken him from an ordinary fisherman to an accused fraudster, and finally to a symbol of the enigmatic nature of the Bermuda Triangle. His days on the open sea continued, each wave seeming to murmur the secrets of that elusive space where normality warps and the improbable becomes everyday.

CHAPTER 12: EBBING FORTUNES

Accusations and Aftermath

Carlos Sanchez, a once-respected fisherman from Bermuda, found himself at the epicenter of an entanglement of scientific skepticism, media scrutiny, and diplomatic tension. He had procured an artifact from the depth of the mysteriously red-tinged waters, an artifact whose elemental composition defied all scientific understanding. Yet, just as inexplicably as it had appeared, the artifact vanished from the high-security lab where it was being analyzed. Accusations burgeoned, pointing fingers at everyone from Carlos to international spies.

The governing bodies overseeing fisheries began to question the legitimacy of Carlos's find, suggesting that he might have orchestrated a grand hoax. Despite his vigorous defense, his fishing license was revoked, citing "questionable conduct" that "could undermine the credibility of marine studies in the region."

Transformations and New Beginnings

As a fisherman, Carlos was a purveyor of reality, his senses honed to navigate the caprices of the ocean. But the scrutiny he faced left him a pariah in his own field, and his boat, which had once brought sustenance to his family, lay idle. But notoriety has its paradoxes. The same enigma that had cost him his livelihood soon offered him an alternative path. The public, fascinated by the

Bermuda Triangle's inexhaustible enigmas, began to view Carlos as a focal point in the ongoing narrative of the Triangle's bizarre phenomena. People speculated on internet forums, conspiracy theorists debated fervently, and soon enough, a bizarre cult of personality emerged around Carlos, bolstering him from vilification to a form of localized fame.

Carlos, seizing the zeitgeist, transitioned into a new role—that of a tour guide specializing in Bermuda Triangle expeditions. His tours were unlike any other; he captivated the audiences with first-hand accounts and pointed out locations where fishermen had returned with tales that intermingled mythology with chilling personal experience. He didn't shun from narrating his own perplexing encounter, which added an extra layer of allure to his expeditions. Though the scientific community distanced itself, the public's fascination with his story became a commercial opportunity, converting his credibility crisis into a lucrative venture.

Diplomacy and International Tensions

The disappearance of the artifact from a secured lab didn't merely cast a shadow over Carlos's life; it also triggered international tensions. Countries with vested interests in oceanographic studies became suddenly alert, cautioning their own researchers about the sensitivity surrounding Bermuda Triangle artifacts. Rumors began to circulate about international spies infiltrating research facilities to gather intelligence, possibly weaponize any findings, or perhaps, as some speculated, to secure the artifact for private collectors whose fascination with the Triangle verged on the obsessive.

The U.S. State Department issued ambiguous statements, both acknowledging the need for scientific transparency and emphasizing the importance of national security.

Governments held closed-door meetings, debating whether the Bermuda Triangle should be internationally recognized as a zone requiring special navigational permissions. Diplomatic complexities escalated, with some countries pushing for greater international oversight, while others argued that such a move would undermine sovereign rights. The artifact had become a geopolitical chess piece, and Carlos, whether he liked it or not, became a figure enmeshed in a narrative much larger than himself.

Summary

Carlos Sanchez's life took a turn of disorienting convolution after his artifact disappeared. His personal life and professional standing were shattered, only to be repurposed in an unexpected manner. He lost his license to fish but gained a new form of livelihood, fulfilling the public's unending appetite for the mysteries of the Bermuda Triangle. Yet, his experience wasn't just a self-contained anomaly; it reverberated on international scales, engendering debates on scientific ethics, national security, and diplomatic jurisdiction. His story, whether deemed a fraud or a genuine enigma, etched itself into the larger, ceaselessly churning saga of the Bermuda Triangle—a region that not only swallows ships and planes but also interpolates the individuals associated with it into a narrative that oscillates between the profoundly personal and the dauntingly global.

CHAPTER 13: STAR-CROSSED

A Cosmic Alignment in Unsettling Waters

Alice's eyes squinted at the telescope as she adjusted its angle, fine-tuning it to the celestial ballet of planets that seemed to coalesce in the night sky. She was an amateur astronomer but no less fervent about her passion than the professionals who devoted their lives to the study. As her cruise ship made its way through the Bermuda Triangle, she thought that the remoteness from land-based light pollution presented an unparalleled opportunity to observe a rare planetary alignment. Venus, Mars, and Jupiter were supposed to intersect at a unique angle, an event that wouldn't happen again for decades. To Alice, this was an unmissable spectacle.

It was a moonless night, and her telescope was perched on the upper deck of the ship, away from the revelry that often occupied such cruises. There was something palpable in the air, an energy she couldn't quite articulate, a serendipity that made her skin tingle with expectation. And then, just as she thought the planets had aligned to their precise positions, a sudden, overwhelming blaze of light erupted from the sky. For a moment, everything was swallowed in a whiteness so intense it seemed almost sentient. She recoiled, her eyes seared by the unexpected luminescence. Before she could fathom what had just transpired, she was enveloped by darkness, as if the universe had blinked and reopened its eyes to find something irrevocably changed.

A Light That Defies Understanding

While Alice was the only one on the ship with a telescope aimed at the heavens, she wasn't the only one to witness the flash of light that briefly transmuted night into day. Other passengers, several of whom were enjoying late-night cocktails or romantic strolls on the deck, became inadvertent witnesses to the inexplicable event. The blinding light was accompanied by a silence that felt almost sacred, a brief pause in the universe's eternal exhalation. People were stunned, disoriented, and a hum of whispers quickly turned into exclamations of astonishment and befuddlement.

When the ship's captain was alerted, his initial concern was that the light was an explosion—perhaps a flare from a ship in distress. Yet no emergency signals came through on any maritime frequencies, and there were no reports of other ships in the immediate area. The onboard meteorologist was equally baffled; no natural atmospheric phenomena could have produced such an intense light devoid of any sound. It was as if for a brief moment, the fundamental laws of physics had been rendered moot, leaving only perplexity in their wake.

Alice was both puzzled and exhilarated, her scientist's mind racing to make sense of what defied all known paradigms. Could it be a natural event unrecorded in scientific annals? Or was it something more esoteric? She reached out to a professor she had kept in touch with from her college days—an astrophysicist with a penchant for the anomalous. He referred her to a controversial paper on "Localized Spacetime Distortions" which posited that under certain rare conditions, celestial alignments could, in theory, distort the fabric of spacetime in their vicinity. The paper was mostly dismissed as speculative fantasy, lacking empirical proof. But what if this was the proof? She couldn't ignore the coincidence of the planetary alignment with the appearance of the strange light.

The Resonance that Lingers

Days after the incident, Alice felt increasingly out of sorts. She developed a sensitivity to light, finding even the subdued lighting of the ship's interior unbearable. When she returned home, medical examinations couldn't explain her condition, though they confirmed a slight degradation of her retinal cells. But more puzzling was her insatiable thirst for understanding what she had witnessed. She scoured academic journals and delved into fringe theories, her fascination with the event bordering on obsession. Conversations with experts left her with more questions than answers. The general consensus was that she had experienced something inexplicable, perhaps even otherworldly, but it remained an enigma wrapped in cosmic conjecture.

The Bermuda Triangle had long been a locus of mysterious happenings, but few could claim a first-hand encounter like Alice's. Whether it was a fortuitous alignment of celestial bodies or something more arcane, the event had left an indelible imprint on her life, forcing her to grapple with questions that science, in its current state, couldn't answer. Just like the mariners and aviators who had entered the Bermuda Triangle's treacherous embrace, she had touched the fringe of something much larger and more incomprehensible than herself. And in that touch, in that brief intersection of her life with the inexplicable, she found a puzzle that her mind, however scientifically inclined, couldn't unravel.

Alice's pursuit of understanding turned her into a somewhat reluctant member of a select community—those who have glimpsed the ungraspable within the Bermuda Triangle and emerged changed, questioning the foundations of their reality. With each question she asked and failed to answer, the mystery only seemed to deepen, forming ripples that extended beyond her, beyond the coordinates of a triangle on a nautical map, into the unfathomable vastness of the universe itself.

CHAPTER 14: HEAVENLY PHENOMENA

In the aftermath of a bewildering celestial spectacle, the cruise liner "Odyssey" navigated choppy seas and an even more unsettled atmosphere among its passengers. Alice Mason, an amateur astronomer who had been observing the singular alignment of Jupiter, Saturn, and Mars, was now the subject of bewilderment herself. The onboard medical facility had become an impromptu base of operations, trying to understand the sudden illness that had overtaken her.

Eyewitness Accounts

Passengers had varying accounts of what transpired, but some elements recurred consistently. A radiance—impossible to describe in any conventional terms—had descended from the sky, casting an ethereal glow upon the ocean. The light lasted for no more than a few seconds, but its effect seemed to linger in the form of an inexplicable sense of euphoria among those who witnessed it. Alice, however, had not been so fortunate.

"For a moment, it was like daylight at midnight," one passenger recounted. "Then Alice screamed, a sound that seemed to come from a place of profound agony. It cut through the awe we were all feeling."

The cruise staff, in their effort to manage the situation, barred further access to Alice, but rumors spread like wildfire. Speculation abounded, from alien encounters to government experiments, and some even whispered about biblical revelations.

The Sudden Illness That Befalls Alice

Alice Mason was far removed from the fray, confined to a sanitized, sterile environment in the ship's medical facility. Despite the application of antipyretics, her fever refused to subside, oscillating between extremes. Adding to the enigma was the manifestation of small, luminous freckles on her arms and face—like constellations embedded in her skin.

Two oceanographers on board, intrigued by the case and with some background in physics, suggested the possibility of Alice experiencing radiation poisoning. They pointed to the luminescent markings as a possible symptom of skin coming into contact with a highly radioactive source. However, their thesis came undone when no other passenger presented with similar symptoms, nor did any Geiger counters on the ship register abnormal levels.

"We've never seen anything like this," admitted Dr. Henry Feldman, the ship's medical officer. "We are not equipped to diagnose, let alone treat, a condition of this sort. We've sent her blood samples to specialized labs, but until we dock, our capabilities are severely limited."

An Obscure Scientific Theory

Dr. Clara Simmons, a particle physicist on sabbatical and also a passenger on the Odyssey, presented a theory so avant-garde it bordered on science fiction. Intrigued by the celestial alignment and the peculiar luminescence, she wondered if Alice had somehow been exposed to a form of cosmic radiation altered by the unique planetary configuration. She posited that Alice had experienced the "Eddington-Finkelstein Transformation."

This hypothetical phenomenon was rooted in General Relativity and quantum mechanics, wherein unique configurations of celestial bodies could, under the right conditions, change the property of cosmic rays or even exotic particles in unknown ways. Such a transformation, if it occurred, could potentially cause effects at the subatomic level, manifesting as unexplained symptoms and anomalies.

Dr. Simmons acknowledged the speculative nature of her theory. "While the Eddington-Finkelstein Transformation is largely theoretical, we cannot entirely discount it. The Bermuda Triangle is replete with phenomena that challenge our understanding of physics and biology. We may have witnessed an intersection of cosmic and earthly oddities, with Alice at the epicenter."

The theory attracted a small but enthusiastic group of proponents among the ship's educated passengers, although skeptics dismissed it as an elaborate rationalization of an event that defied logical scrutiny. Conversations grew more polarized, academic debates took on the fervor of ideological clashes, and the tale of Alice Mason's extraordinary experience became an inextricable part of Bermuda Triangle lore.

As the ship approached its port of call, the gravity of Alice's predicament became clear: her condition was not improving, and no conventional diagnosis could be made. The mysteries of what she had undergone—whether astronomical, physical, or metaphysical—loomed large, a subject of vehement discourse and private wonder.

The questions remained—what had Alice experienced and at what cost? Had she become a conduit for celestial energies unknown to science? Had she stumbled upon a form of enlightenment or a cosmic warning? Or was her ordeal merely a confluence of chance events that conspired to create an inexplicable medical and cosmic enigma? Amid debates and theories, one truth was incontrovertible: Alice Mason had sailed into the Bermuda Triangle an amateur astronomer and emerged an enigma, a woman touched or perhaps even marked by the heavens themselves.

CHAPTER 15: EARTHLY CONSEQUENCES

The Metamorphosis of Perception

Alice navigated through a world that had gone dark but seemed to have illuminated her other senses. The loss of her vision was not a condition doctors could adequately diagnose, let alone treat. In the plethora of medical jargon, from retinopathy to occipital lobe malfunction, none of the experts had a convincing explanation for what had happened to her in the Bermuda Triangle. The celestial phenomenon, the sudden burst of light—these had been relegated to the realm of unverified theories and idle speculation.

Her other senses, however, began to sharpen in a manner that was tantamount to an evolutionary leap. She could hear the gentle rustling of autumn leaves from a mile away, feel the atmospheric pressure change before a thunderstorm, and taste the subtlest nuances in her meals—flavors she'd never noticed before. These heightened perceptions didn't merely compensate for her loss; they granted her a different manner of "seeing" the world around her.

The Losses and Gains

Alice's professional life as a physicist took a devastating hit. The academic community expressed empathy, but empathy didn't hold up to the rigors of scientific research. Her career was predicated on data, algorithms, and computer models—all of which she could no longer directly interact with. The university eventually severed its ties with her, couched in polite legalese that couldn't mask the cruel finality of the situation.

However, as doors closed, windows opened in ways she hadn't anticipated. Alice's story resonated with people, not merely as a cautionary tale about the perils of the Bermuda Triangle, but as an embodiment of resilience in the face of inconceivable adversity. Invitations to speak at various platforms began to pour in. At first, these speaking engagements were dominated by questions about the mysterious incident—questions she had no satisfactory answers to. Over time, the conversations shifted to the topic of resilience and adaptability. She found herself transitioning from a physicist to a motivational speaker, focusing on adaptation and finding strength in life's inexplicable challenges.

The Enigmatic Symbiosis of Science and Spirituality

One of the more fascinating dimensions of Alice's new life was her strange relationship with science and spirituality—a relationship characterized by tension and paradox. Alice had always been rooted in empiricism, but her experience in the Bermuda Triangle and its aftermath thrust her into an ontological quandary. There was no empirical explanation for her heightened senses or for the mysterious celestial event itself. On the other hand, the sudden acuity of her remaining senses could not be entirely relegated to spirituality or mysticism; they were real, physiological changes, yet to be fully understood by science.

This led her to explore neuroplasticity, the brain's ability to adapt by reorganizing itself, and its possible connections to her new sensory capabilities. While she couldn't participate in laboratory research, she collaborated with neuroscientists who were eager to explore her condition. Meanwhile, spirituality became an integral part of her motivational talks, not as a religious dictum, but as an open question about the limits of human understanding and the profundity of experiences that defy logical explanation.

Summing Up the Journey

In the years following her encounter in the Bermuda Triangle, Alice led a life that was both inspiring and perplexing. Her professional landscape had radically altered, from the observatory telescopes aimed at celestial bodies to auditorium microphones aimed at soul-searching audiences.

She hadn't found a way to reconcile her scientific background with the unexplainable phenomenon she had experienced, and that was alright. For her, this episode was a lesson in embracing uncertainty, in understanding that not everything could be neatly categorized or understood. While she may have lost her sight, Alice had gained something equally significant: an expansive, nuanced perspective that allowed her to navigate life's complexities in ways she had never imagined possible.

The Bermuda Triangle had taken something from her, but it had also granted her something ineffable, something that eluded straightforward classification. Just like the enigmatic waters that altered her life forever, Alice embodied a mystery that was both confounding and deeply inspiring. And as she stepped onto yet another stage, ready to share her story, she knew she was a living testament to the adaptability and resilience of the human spirit —a journey that was as mysterious and profound as the Bermuda Triangle itself.

CHAPTER 16: A QUIET PRELUDE

On the Cusp of Silence

Ian Anderson, an accomplished musician known for his intricate compositions, had always been intrigued by the transcendent power of sound. Now, on a yacht cutting through the azure expanses of the Bermuda Triangle, he hoped for nothing more than a rejuvenating escape from his hectic life. Surrounded by friends who admired both his talent and his insatiable curiosity, he imagined a weekend of simple pleasures: reading, swimming, and perhaps a bit of impromptu music-making.

As evening settled, Ian took a walk on the deck to breathe in the sea air. But then, it happened. A melody, the likes of which he had never heard before, seeped into his ears. It was both ephemeral and penetrating, as if woven from the threads of dreams and reality. Entranced, he hurried to his cabin to grab his smartphone, intent on capturing the fleeting notes.

The instrumentality of the melody was indescribable. It was a soundscape, not merely a tune—an auditory texture that seemed to emanate from every direction, as though the ocean and sky were its instruments. Hands shaking, he activated the voice recorder on his phone and raised it to capture the haunting timbre.

But the moment he pressed the record button, he felt a surge of vertigo that overwhelmed his senses. His vision blurred, and before he knew what was happening, he fainted, collapsing onto the deck with his phone still clutched in his hand.

An Unsettling Investigation

Ian regained consciousness to find himself surrounded by worried faces. His friends had found him lying on the deck and had called the ship's medic. Upon explaining what he had heard, the others admitted they'd heard nothing out of the ordinary. Intrigued and slightly alarmed, Ian replayed the voice recording, but all it presented was static, as if his smartphone had failed to capture any sound.

"I swear I heard it; it was unlike anything I've ever experienced. A symphony from nowhere, a melody without origin," he insisted, his voice tinged with a combination of excitement and distress.

His friends recommended he get some rest, attributing his experience to fatigue or possibly a hallucination. Still, Ian was not convinced. That night, he scoured the internet, diving into forums and scientific papers concerning the acoustic anomalies sometimes reported within the Bermuda Triangle. Though he found no accounts identical to his own, he stumbled upon some mentions of sounds—sometimes called "skyquakes" or "mistpouffers"—that had similarly eluded explanation.

Intricacies and Absurdities

The yacht returned to port the next day, and Ian found himself obsessively reviewing the details of his experience. He knew he needed professional insight, so he reached out to some of the leading experts in acoustics and soundscapes. Their responses were mixed; some entertained the idea of an unexplored acoustic phenomenon, possibly connected to atmospheric or oceanic conditions, while others outright dismissed Ian's account as the result of auditory hallucination or a technological malfunction.

Fueling further skepticism, law enforcement got involved. Word had gotten out about Ian's mysterious encounter in the Triangle, and there were murmurs of possible foul play. Ian was questioned about his activities on the yacht, the substances he had consumed, and his mental health background. It was a demoralizing process, one that felt like an affront to his integrity and his professional reputation.

Defiant yet befuddled, Ian couldn't shake off the celestial harmony that had graced his ears, as if granting him a brief audience with the ineffable. The melody stayed with him, becoming a lingering motif in his thoughts, an enigmatic riddle that begged for resolution yet defied all logical inquiry.

For some, Ian's Bermuda Triangle encounter cast a dubious light on his reputation. Questions were raised about his credibility, and some even questioned his mental state. But for others, it became a matter of intrigue, another enigmatic piece in the complex jigsaw puzzle of unexplained phenomena linked to the Bermuda Triangle.

The melody he had heard became a silenced part of him, like a ghost note in a complex musical arrangement, invisible yet profoundly affecting. It was a silent prelude to a life-altering transformation, one that would leave him questioning the very fabric of his reality, his profession, and his understanding of the world's acoustic phenomena.

The ramifications of that mysterious evening in the Bermuda Triangle would forever alter Ian's life, leaving him in a state of existential disquietude, haunted by a melody without source, and surrounded by a silence that was far from empty. Indeed, the aftershock of his uncanny experience would ripple through the years, leaving indelible marks on his psyche and career—effects that were as perplexing as they were profound. Ian Anderson had touched the untouchable, heard the unhearable, and in doing so, he had crossed an ineffable boundary, one that lies beyond scientific explanation and ventures into the realms of the mysterious and the uncharted.

CHAPTER 17: NOTES IN THE VOID

The inexplicable events surrounding Ian and his enigmatic experience with the elusive melody had left an indelible impact not only on him but also on those who attempted to fathom this phenomenon. The ordeal traversed the corridors of science, calling into question our understanding of acoustics and resonance, and wading into the murkier waters of clandestine scrutiny by law enforcement.

The Enigma of Resonance

Ian's initial attempt to record the mysterious melody was not wholly unsuccessful, even though he had fainted in the process. The equipment he had with him did capture something—though what it captured became a matter of debate among experts in acoustic science and cryptography alike. The recorded sounds lacked coherent musical structure but fluctuated in frequency and amplitude in a way that was both mathematically chaotic and eerily systematic. Dr. Lillian Margrove, a leading researcher in acoustic anomalies, pointed out that, "The sound patterns do not align with any natural phenomena we know of, nor do they fit the principles of man-made compositions. It's as though we're hearing a language we can't yet comprehend."

A Symphony of Scrutiny

Skeptics questioned the authenticity of the incident, propelling law enforcement agencies to involve themselves. Suspicion arose that Ian may have staged an elaborate hoax, perhaps to create publicity for an upcoming musical project or to serve some darker, undisclosed agenda. The involvement of authorities was unsettling and paradoxical; they were seeking tangible evidence in a situation that defied empirical constraints.

After an exhaustive search of Ian's yacht and thorough forensic analysis of his recording equipment, nothing unusual was detected. All machinery functioned within normal parameters, and nothing on board could have created the sounds captured. Forensic audio analysts who scoured the recording found no signs of tampering. Despite this, law enforcement officials remained cautious, their interest piqued but not satisfied. "We can't rule out the possibility of ulterior motives," warned Detective Harold Finch, "but we also can't ignore the unexplainable. For now, it remains an open inquiry."

Expert Testimonies and Wider Implications

The mysterious melody not only confused forensic experts but also puzzled scholars of ethnomusicology and cultural anthropology. They were unable to classify it within the paradigms of any known musical tradition. Dr. Henrietta Leung, a music theorist specializing in the evolution of musical scales, commented that the melody, "Engages with a kind of tonality that exists outside of Western, Eastern, or any other conventional systems. Its intricacies are perplexing, if not outright disconcerting."

Subsequent attempts to replicate the conditions of Ian's experience were conducted under controlled environments but yielded no results. Researchers tried to recreate the specific location, timing, and meteorological conditions to no avail. Other musicians and sound engineers who sailed to the exact coordinates could not capture anything out of the ordinary, leaving the scientific community baffled. Dr. Margrove concluded, "The more we delve into it, the more it seems as if the melody chose to reveal itself exclusively to Ian, which is both fascinating and disconcerting."

Though investigations did not yield a clear conclusion, the inquiries inadvertently opened up new avenues of interdisciplinary research. If nothing else, Ian's unexplainable experience exposed limitations in our understanding of both natural phenomena and the intricacies of human perception. Scientific journals and forums buzzed with debates ranging from the limitations of sound engineering to the enigmas of deep-sea acoustic corridors and even the possibilities of a previously unknown form of communication—either terrestrial or perhaps, chillingly, extraterrestrial. As for Ian, who had become the unwitting nucleus of this spiraling enigma, the scrutiny and the unanswered questions only intensified the profound isolation he felt since that fateful voyage.

In the absence of any clear answers, Ian's melody remains an enigma—a sonorous anomaly echoing in the intellectual void, challenging our understanding of the very fabric of reality and the limits of human cognition. The realm of known science had been disrupted, and in the unsettling quietude that followed, many were left to wonder: How many more uncharted symphonies await us in the Bermuda Triangle's inscrutable depths? And, perhaps more hauntingly, are we prepared for the revelations they may bring?

CHAPTER 18: CODA IN SOLITUDE

The ripples Ian's experience in the Bermuda Triangle set off were nothing short of transformative. It wasn't just that he lost his hearing, a tragedy for anyone but an existential cataclysm for a musician. It was how that loss forced him into uncharted creative territories, places he would never have ventured otherwise. If the mysterious melody he heard on that yacht was the prologue to a new life, then the unfolding chapters were nothing like what he— or anyone else—could have anticipated.

The Silent Realm of Cinema

Retreating from the public eye, Ian submerged himself in a kind of hermitic existence. But he was far from idle. Within the quietude of his studio, transformed into a miniaturized film set, he devoted himself to an entirely different art form: silent films.

It was a curious irony that silent films, once a relic of the early 20th century, became his new medium. Yet, with meticulous frame-by-frame craftsmanship, Ian began to produce works of astonishing depth and subtlety, narrative jewels that could convey a spectrum of human emotions without uttering a single word. The poignancy of these works resonated across international film festivals. Film critics, often skeptical of ventures by celebrities in different artistic arenas, unanimously hailed Ian as an auteur to be reckoned with.

The films often focused on the mysteries of human existence, laced with themes that were patently uncanny. Some even dared to speculate whether Ian's works were a cryptic retelling of his own Bermuda Triangle experience. However, Ian remained tight-lipped about such conjectures, further fueling the sense of enigma around him.

The Academic and Artistic Enigma

While Ian's auditory faculties had been severed, his career found an unexpected but nonetheless distinguished renaissance in academia. Universities and film schools were keen to dissect his work, which led to scholarly articles, thesis papers, and even dedicated courses that explored the motifs and narrative techniques employed in his silent films. Notable philosophers and semioticians dissected his films, commenting on the peculiar synesthesia that they induced, a transmutation of visual storytelling into an almost auditory experience.

Ian's newfound status also led to invitations for guest lectures. Even without the capability to hear the questions from the audience, Ian's insightful, typewritten answers, projected onto a screen, were enough to hold auditoriums spellbound. When asked what motivated him to choose silent films, Ian's reply was as enigmatic as ever: "Silence, after all, has a quality of sound that is only heard by those who listen."

An Enigmatic Coda

The art form he embraced turned out to be Ian's coda in life. He never returned to music, at least not in the conventional sense. Yet, the symphony of his existence found new notes, new chords, and new crescendos, albeit in a different kind of auditorium. His works became legendary, often considered pieces of philosophical meditation as much as they were pieces of art. However, the enigmatic melodies that once led him to this peculiar transformation never made it to any form of recorded media. Law enforcement agencies had long shelved the case, unable to discern any form of foul play or definitive evidence.

Ian continued to be reclusive, keeping his public appearances to a minimum. Yet, rumors abounded. Some claimed he was working on an opus, a masterwork that would finally bring to light the experiences that led him to renounce his earlier art form. Yet, others believe that the music he once heard still echoes in the confines of his mind, an ineffable experience that transcends any form of earthly expression.

In an existence paradoxically shaped by sound and silence, Ian found a unique kind of peace, a solitude that wasn't lonely but profoundly full. Whether it was a blessing or a curse, a form of ascension or an abyss, the jury is still out. But one thing is certain: Ian's art became his echo in the world, a sonic imprint not in the form of decibels but in the indelible impact he left on those who experienced his work.

There was no clear resolution to the mysterious circumstances that enveloped his Bermuda Triangle journey. Yet, they compelled a prodigious transformation that neither Ian nor the world could ignore. If the Bermuda Triangle was a realm of baffling anomalies and inexplicable phenomena, then Ian's life, in its own way, became an undeciphered sonata, written in notes that perhaps, only he could hear.

CONCLUSION

In cartography, the Bermuda Triangle's coordinates are well-defined. It is an area bounded by Miami, Bermuda, and Puerto Rico—a 500,000 square mile expanse often maligned as a locale of inexplicable phenomena. But beyond these mathematical certainties, the stories you've encountered stretch the boundaries of our empirical knowledge and delve into the enigmatic spectra of human experiences. Indeed, the real mystery of the Bermuda Triangle is not about geographical locations or navigational bearings, but the enigmatic transformations undergone by those who have had the audacity to intrude upon its veiled sanctity.

A Transmutation of Self

The chronicles unfold not merely as a series of baffling events but as transformative moments, crucibles that have forever altered the lives of those involved. William, the experienced pilot, did not just vanish; he left behind a labyrinthine void that his son has pledged to traverse. The story shifted from the inexplicable loss of a plane to a familial drama built upon endless questions and relentless pursuits. Likewise, Emily, the marine biologist, metamorphosed from a devoted scientist to a spiritual maverick, finding an almost mystical relationship with the ocean, even as she sacrificed her professional standing. Each narrative diverges from a point of inscrutability into complex paradigms of human resilience, vulnerabilities, and the myriad ways in which people adapt to incomprehensible situations.

The Hidden Currents of Reality

In the whirlpool that Tom and Linda encountered, we find an extraordinary metaphor for the temporal distortions that punctuate our existence. Time, a supposedly fixed coordinate, was scrambled, leaving the couple at odds with their own reality and each other. This sense of dislocation is not merely geographical; it's a rend in the fabric of their lives, echoing in fractured relationships and altered futures. Carlos, too, found his life upended. What began as an enigmatic artifact led him to navigate murky geopolitical tensions and unfathomable public scrutiny. While he lost one form of livelihood, he found another as a guide in the abyss of uncertainty that the Bermuda Triangle represents.

The Penumbral Frontier

The Bermuda Triangle is a space that exists in the dim penumbra between scientific rigor and the mists of the uncharted. Alice's celestial alignment and Ian's silent sonata are testaments to the zone's defiance of empirical norms. What are we to make of an astronomer who finds illumination in the loss of sight or a musician who finds expression in the absence of sound? Their experiences suggest that the Bermuda Triangle is more than a place—it's an intermediary realm, a metaphorical domain where the inexplicable is not only encountered but internalized, transforming mere observers into complex vessels of contradictory truths.

The lessons extracted from these six tales converge on a singular point: The Bermuda Triangle is not merely a geographic entity, it is a conceptual vortex, an ontological challenge that disrupts our standard modes of understanding and forces us to confront the existential anomalies latent in the human condition. By traversing this elusive realm, each individual does not simply cross geographical coordinates; they traverse boundaries of understanding, realms of consciousness, and landscapes of self-perception. The very landscape of the Bermuda Triangle stands as an indelible allegory for the liminal spaces in our own lives

—spaces that reside between certainty and doubt, logic and emotion, reality and the unimaginable.

It is these internal voyages, compelled by encounters with the unknowable, that we must ultimately map. In pondering the narratives herein, you are urged to consider not just the enigma of the Bermuda Triangle but the deeper riddles of existence that lie within the triangulations of your own experience. It serves as a mirror reflecting back our human longing to explore, understand, and make sense of the mysteries that reside not just in the corners of the world, but in the unfathomed depths of the human spirit. It challenges us to consider: What coordinates do we live by, and what mysteries lie just beyond the periphery of our understanding, daring us to venture beyond?

THE END

Printed in Great Britain
by Amazon